The Prophet's Blueprint:
The Comprehensive Study
Guide

by

Jeremy Lopez

The Prophet's Blueprint: The Comprehensive
Study Guide

By Dr. Jeremy Lopez
Copyright © 2020

Published by Identity Network
P.O. Box 38213
Birmingham, AL 35238
www.IdentityNetwork.net

ENDORSEMENTS

You are put on this earth with incredible potential and a divine destiny. This powerful, practical man shows you how to tap into power you didn't even know you had. – Brian Tracy – Author, *The Power of Self Confidence*

I found myself savoring the concepts of the Law of Attraction merging with the Law of Creativity until slowly the beautiful truths seeped deeper into my thirsty soul. I am called to be a Creator! My friend, Dr. Jeremy Lopez, has a way of reminding us of our eternal 'I-Am-ness' while putting the tools in our hands to unlock our endless creative potential with the Divine mind. As a musical composer, I'm excited to explore, with greater understanding, the infinite realm of possibilities as I place fingers on my piano and whisper, 'Let there be!'

– Dony McGuire, Grammy Award winning artist and musical composer

Jeremy dives deep into the power of consciousness and shows us that we can create a world where the champion within us can shine and how we can manifest our desires to live a life of fulfillment. A must read! – Greg S. Reid – Forbes and Inc. top rated Keynote Speaker

I have been privileged to know Jeremy Lopez for many years, as well as sharing the platform with him at a number of conferences. Through this time, I have

found him as a man of integrity, commitment, wisdom, and one of the most networked people I have met. Jeremy is an entrepreneur and a leader of leaders. He has amazing insights into leadership competencies and values. He has a passion to ignite this latent potential within individuals and organizations and provide ongoing development and coaching to bring about competitive advantage and success. I would highly recommend him as a speaker, coach, mentor, and consultant. – Chris Gaborit – Learning Leader, Trainer

CONTENTS

INTRODUCTION

Throughout my life and years in public ministry, I have been so very privileged to have ministered to heads of business, heads of state, as well as to celebrities of the stage and screen, speaking prophetically into their lives and giving them direction, counsel and insight. Through it all, what I have come to realize that the prophetic gift is just alive and well today as ever it was before. The gift never ceased. It never ended. The age of the prophet never changed or vanished form the earth. Today, as never before, humanity is hungering after a greater measure of the supernatural. Day in and day out, seeker, just like you, are coming into contact with the Presence of God and realizing that within them lies a very powerful energy to shape the future and to call things into existence - a power to create.

Like me, you, too, are a creator. You always have been. When I felt the inspiration of the Holy Spirit to write The Prophet's Blueprint: The Etymology of Prophecy, I first felt the immense weight and responsibility to share with the world the truth concerning the invisible world within - the realm of the Kingdom. I also felt a sense of passionate fervor to share, as never before, the behind-the-scenes of the actual mechanics at work within the realm of the prophetic. As I have asked before, does God truly do everything for us? Does God bring His own Word to pass? And, if so, what role, if any, are we as believers to play in bringing about the manifestation of our own prophetic promises? Are we to simply believe, to trust, and to hope? Are we to sit casually upon the sidelines of life, waiting and wishing for change to come? Or is there, instead, some other role that we've been offered to play? As you read my newest book, The Prophet's Blueprint: The Etymology of Prophecy, my prayer for you is that you would begin to see and to understand as never before that the call to prophesy is also a call to create – a call to shape the world and a call to change destinies. Long, long before you ever came to this earth, you existed, in the beginning, with God. You were there. And so was I. We were known by Him, long before we were ever formed within the wombs of our mothers. And, even then, there were plans in place. When writing the book, I felt inspired by the Holy Spirit to share in great detail, insight into the mechanics of prophecy, delving more deeply than ever before into the topic of the prophetic. As a minister and prophet to the nations, what I have found and continue to see more and more, day in and day out, is that we have been given a role to play in the manifestation of every prophetic promise. No, you have not been called to simply sit by and wait. While you are waiting, there is also a very real, very divine role in which you have been cast. As a co-creator with God, possessing within your own physical body the energy of Creation, you have been a very specific task – an assignment. This assignment existed for you long, long before time ever was. And those plans that existed, they are part of the divine assignment. You see, my friend and fellow seeker, you have been programmed to prophesy. That is to say, specifically, you have been programmed to bring those plans into manifestation. Suffice it to say, you have been programmed to prosper. Those thoughts and those plans that existed in the very Beginning – long, long before time ever even began, those plans are good plans. Those thoughts are good thoughts. The time has come to answer the call. The time has come to bring about every dream and desire.

SECTION ONE

DISPENSATION?

Though I speak with the tongues of men and of angels, and have not charity, I am become as sounding brass, or a tinkling cymbal.

2 And though I have the gift of prophecy, and understand all mysteries, and all knowledge; and though I have all faith, so that I could remove mountains, and have not charity, I am nothing.

3 And though I bestow all my goods to feed the poor, and though I give my body to be burned, and have not charity, it profiteth me nothing.

4 Charity suffereth long, and is kind; charity envieth not; charity vaunteth not itself, is not puffed up,

5 Doth not behave itself unseemly, seeketh not her own, is not easily provoked, thinketh no evil;

6 Rejoiceth not in iniquity, but rejoiceth in the truth;

7 Beareth all things, believeth all things, hopeth all things, endureth all things.

8 Charity never faileth: but whether there be prophecies, they shall fail; whether there be tongues, they shall cease; whether there be knowledge, it shall vanish away.

9 For we know in part, and we prophesy in part.

10 But when that which is perfect is come, then that which is in part shall be done away.

11 When I was a child, I spake as a child, I understood as a child, I thought as a child: but when I became a man, I put away childish things.

12 For now we see through a glass, darkly; but then face to face: now I know in part; but then shall I know even as also I am known.

13 And now abideth faith, hope, charity, these three; but the greatest of these is charity. (1 Corinthians 13:1-13 KJV)

It seems so straight-forward and so matter-of-fact, doesn't it? It seems, at least according to the words of the Apostle Paul, that a time will come when prophecy will cease – when the prophetic gift will simply become silent and no longer needed. For centuries, there have been many of the persuasion that prophecy existed only for a certain time and a certain season – for a certain dispensation. Some, in fact, believe that prophecies already have ceased – that the gift ceased centuries ago. As you journey through the pages of my newest book, The Prophet's Blueprint: The Etymology of Prophecy, my hope is that you take a journey through time, also, back to the ancient days when the words of prophets shaped and helped to define the destinies of kings and kingdoms. Etymology, in fact, by definition, is a discovery of origins. Somewhere along the way, it seems, many within the modern Body of Christ have lost sight of the truth regarding prophecy. Prophecy, to most, is little more than some gift of predicting the future. As a result, all too often, the modern prophetic movement throughout the world has lost its much of its power, becoming relegated to little more than cheapened clichés and innuendo, rather than being the catalyst by which mankind is propelled into the awakening of its own innate power – the power of the Godhead residing bodily, which is the power to create worlds.

You see, my friend, somewhere along the way, because of the damnable lies of religious orthodoxy, we have resigned ourselves to believe that somewhere long ago the voice of the prophet changed in some way or that it became less valid or less relevant. Faulty and erroneous teachings, in part, mixed with the erroneous theology of dispensationalism has left many a sincere believer questioning even the validity of the prophetic voice. And, as a result, a sort of double-mindedness has crept into the Church as a whole. We say that we believe in prophecy; yet, for the most part, resign ourselves to the sidelines of life, waiting, wishing, and hoping for fulfillment to come to pass, rather than becoming active participants in the prophetic manifestation. The early church and, in fact, those prophets of ancient times, regarded prophecy not as some tool of prediction but, rather, as a tool for creation. We find these accounts recorded all throughout the sacred writings of the Holy Bible and also in various other world religious texts. Prophecy, in truth, is not a religious concept but is rather a very human concept. Where there is the ability to dream and to imagine and to cast vision, there exists also the ability to prophesy. Whether you have ever taken the time to realize it or not, you have always been prophesying something according to your thoughts and the beliefs you hold to. It is time to become much more aware of the power you possess to create the world around you and this begins by coming to a better, more comprehensive understanding of the role of prophecy throughout the ages. Cessationist theology holds to the belief that the gifts of the Holy Spirit existed solely within the First Century Church and that such gifts ceased to be at the end of the life of the last Apostle John.

Cassationsists hold to the view that the gifts of the Holy Spirit were given solely to the Early Church solely for the purpose of ushering in the Apostolic Age – and that there is currently now no need for miracles, signs, or wonders any longer. Cassationists hold to the writings of the Apostle Paul in his epistle to the Corinthian church to back up this erroneous claim, citing, often, "Paul said that prophecies would cease." The reality, however, is that prophecy, itself, has never ceased. In fact, never has there ever been a time in which the prophetic voice has been silent – although it may have at times seemed so.

Historically speaking, there is much to be said about the role of prophecy within the early church - particularly the church within its infantile stage within the first three centuries. Origen, an early church father and theologian, had much to say regarding the role of prophecy and also the over all working of the Holy Spirit within the early apostolic church. In his work, titled, Contra Celsum, Origen notes that many of the miracles which were once so prevalent in the early days of the church following Pentecost had begun to greatly diminish, stating that signs of the "Paraclete" had all but vanished. That is, except prophecy. Even at a time when the early church found itself in league with the powerful, political forces of the Roman Empire, there were those, still, who prophesied. And, even as other notable signs and wonders seemed to diminish, the voice of the prophets still prevailed - even in times of social, political, and religious upheaval.

Could it be that many regard the words of Origen to mean that the gifts existed solely for a specific time and for a certain dispensation? Could it be that Cessationist theology originates because of the writings of Origen? Furthermore, could it be that the words of Origen have been greatly misunderstood for centuries?

Henry Chadwick, when writing his book researching the work of Origen, writes, "Few works of the early Church are as interesting to the modern reader or as important to the historian as Origen's reply to the attack on Christianity made by the pagan Celsus. The Contra Celsum is the culmination of the great apologetic movement of the Second and Third centuries AD, and is for the Greek Church what St Augustine's City of God is for Western Christendom. It is also one of the chief monuments of the coming together of ancient Greek culture and the new faith of the expanding Christian society. Thus, Origen's work is of interest not only to the historian and theologian, but also to the Hellenist."

You see, my friend and fellow seeker, it was never that the signs of the Holy Spirit ever truly vanished or diminished. The gifts never ceased. Where the Holy Spirit is, there, too, are the gifts. For, as Paul wrote to the early church, the gifts are subject to the Spirit Himself, to use as He wills. However, in a time of political upheaval, following the fall of Jerusalem in 70 AD, there were moments of time in which the gifts became silenced - save, the gift of prophecy. We find, historically speaking, that even when other gifts seemed to be nonexistent, even then, the role of the prophet was alive and well. We find this confirmed even in the writings contained within the Didache - the teachings of the first century church - outlining the role of the prophet within the early church. Never, truly, has the gift of prophecy ever been silenced and never has the prophetic gift ever ceased from existence. Where the Spirit of the Lord is, there, too, is the ability to prophesy. And where there exists the prophetic unction, so, too, does there exist the power to create worlds.

SECTION TWO

SELF-FULFILLMENT

Marisa T. Cohen Ph.D., CPLC, author of Finding Love: The Scientific Take, writes for Psychology Today in an article titled Self-Fulfilling Prophecy Can Our Beliefs Force the End of our Relationship? A self-fulfilling prophecy occurs when our beliefs influence our behaviors. An example of this would be: If we predict that we will fail at a certain task, such as giving a speech, and subsequently wind up stumbling through it. In such a situation, our belief seems to get the best of us, and we act in ways that affirm it.

Research has also tied the self-fulfilling prophecy to relationships. Our expectations about the successes/failures in our relationships can influence their outcomes. Downey, Freitas, Michaelis, and Khouri (1998) carried out two studies to determine if people's expectations of rejection would prompt them to behave in ways that lead to the demise of these relationships. The authors were also interested in how self-fulfilling prophecy affects people who score high in rejection sensitivity (RS).

In their first study, members of couples recorded their cognitions, affects, behaviors, and conflicts in daily diary entries. A total of 108 heterosexual couples who had been dating for at least six months were used for this study.

Diary analysis was carried out for the 58 couples who completed the study and filled out entries for four weeks. One year after the study, all of the original couples were contacted again for a follow-up to see if they had broken up.

Participants were initially given a demographic questionnaire, the Rejection Sensitivity Questionnaire, and measures of relationship satisfaction and commitment. Results demonstrated that 44% percent of couples that included a woman who was high in rejection sensitivity (HRS) had broken up at the one-year follow-up, compared to 15% of couples that included a woman who was low in rejection sensitivity (LRS) (Downey et al., 1998).

With regard to men, 42% of couples that included a man with a high level of rejection sensitivity broke up at the one-year mark, whereas 15% of couples with a man with a low level of rejection sensitivity broke up. Downey et al. (1998) reported that "...the effect of people's RS on breakup remained significant when their partners' RS, relationship satisfaction, and commitment assessed prior to beginning the diary study were statistically controlled..." (p. 549). The researchers also found out that the couples that broke up were more dissatisfied at the daily level over the course of the study. Downey et al. (1998) also examined if reports of relationship satisfaction and desire to end the relationship were related to reports of conflict that occurred during the previous day, and if satisfaction and desire to break up were related to rejection sensitivity. While nothing was shown for the men, there was a significant difference amongst the women. Partners of women with a high level of rejection sensitivity differed from the partners of those with low level of rejection sensitivity on days that were preceded by conflict. The partners of those women high in RS reported more dissatisfaction and were much more likely to think about ending the relationship the day after the conflict. Women who were high in rejection sensitivity were also much less likely to view their partners as accepting the day after conflict than those low in RS. Overall, the authors found that rejection sensitivity was a self-fulfilling prophecy in that it predicted breakup. Of course, this is because they were in high conflict situations that activated their expectations.

Downey et al. (1998) note, "… that naturally occurring conflicts triggered a process through which women's rejection expectancies led to their partners' rejecting responses, operationalized as partner-reported relationship dissatisfaction and thoughts of ending the relationship. Both of these indexes of rejection predicted breakup for men and for women" (p. 553). A noteworthy limitation was the self-report nature of the diaries. Additionally, perceptions were not assessed immediately after the conflict so the male responses the day after the conflict are difficult to clearly understand.

In a follow-up study aimed at addressing the limitations of the first study, 39 college-aged exclusive couples participated and were videotaped. Results demonstrated that the partners of HRS and LRS women did not differ before the conflict but differed after conflict. Specifically, partners of women high in rejection sensitivity were angrier about their relationships after the conflict. Interestingly, post-conflict, there was a nonsignificant increase in the anger of the male partners of HRS women, but a significant decline in the partners of LRS women. The HRS women were also shown to behave more negatively during the conflict.

Caution must be taken when interpreting the study in that perceptions were explored, not actual behaviors. In addition, results demonstrated that the expectations of HRS women led to the relationship ending as a result of less satisfaction and commitment on the part of their partners. However, the actual nature in which the relationships ended was not explored. For example, the authors note that the HRS women may have become so dissatisfied with the accumulation of perceived rejection that they ended the relationship, or that they ended the relationship preemptively to avoid perceived rejection (Downey et al., 1998).

Clifford N. Lazarus Ph.D., wrote for Psychology Today, in an article titled, How to Stop Self-Fulfilling Prophecies of Failure, "Mike dreaded an impending sales report he was scheduled to present to the department. Although the report was glowing with profit and efficiency,

Mike was convinced that he couldn't "step up" and would make a fool of himself when delivering it. He was so nervous on the day of his presentation that he claimed to be feeling ill and went home from work. "This proves it!" he thought to himself, "I really am a loser."

A "self-fulfilling prophecy" is when one predicts an outcome and then inadvertently acts in a way that brings about the very result predicted. Usually, the term denotes the creation of negative or unfortunate events, such as failure or disappointment, or unpleasant emotional reactions, such as anxiety, anger or depression. And, because many of these undesirable outcomes tend to build on themselves and gather momentum, they often become cycles –

what most of us think of as "vicious circles."

Of course, not all self-fulfilling prophecies are negative or undesirable because some produce "virtuous circles" wherein positive predictions lead one to act in ways that achieve desired outcomes. Nevertheless, this post focuses on self-fulfilling prophecies that result in undesirable or self-defeating cycles.

In most cases, these negative cycles start with deep-seated negative and irrational beliefs, ideas, or expectations about oneself, other people, or the world. Such firmly entrenched negative beliefs are usually the product of upbringing and previous experiences and are often implanted by significant people and events.

For example, if someone grows up hearing from his or her parents that he or she is "stupid," "incapable," "bad," or "unworthy," after a while, the negative indoctrination will probably take hold and the unfortunate person will start to believe these uncomplimentary and basically inaccurate notions.

Once in place, these core negative beliefs start to give rise to a variety of equally uncharitable, irrational thoughts and expectations that take the form of negative self-talk and unpleasant mental pictures. In short, if you believe you are bad, you will probably go around thinking and imagining bad things about yourself.

These negative thoughts and images, in turn, create a host of negative emotional states such as anger, depression, anxiety, guilt, and shame. Naturally, if you are bogged down in bad feelings, it's difficult to do things well or engage in adaptive behavior. And as a result, your actions may include social withdrawal, avoidance, dishonesty, aggression, and even drug and alcohol abuse.

The cycle continues: If you are behaving negatively, actual undesirable outcomes are likely to happen. Poor performance, interpersonal problems, and even failure, divorce, and drug dependence can result. And the occurrence of these actual, negative outcomes serves to drive the entire cycle full circle by reinforcing the very core negative beliefs that started it off in the first place!

So, what can be done to break the cycle of these negative self-fulfilling prophecies? The solution is based on corrective thinking and corrective action.

Corrective thinking aims to uncover the core irrational beliefs and replace negative self-talk and upsetting mental pictures with more rational and accurate thoughts, images and expectations.

Corrective action encourages people to master challenges by confronting problems instead of avoiding or denying them.

In essence, if you learn coping strategies today, you will be better off tomorrow no matter how upset you were yesterday.

Remember: Think well, Act well, Feel well, Be well!"

Could it be that somewhere along the way, where our own thoughts and beliefs are concerned, we've limited our very own selves to believing that we have no real say in the matters of life and that we're simply being driven by the winds of chance? Could it be that for far too long, we've said, "Whatever will be will be," forgetting that we've always had a very real, all-important role to play within all matters of life? As you know by now, you are a powerful creator, having been filled with all the powers of the Godhead. You are a creator not only with God within the heavenly realms but also within all matters of your own day to day life. As it's so often said, whether you think you can or you think you can't, you're right! It really is so very true. Even as the scriptures remind us, as a man thinketh, so is he!

But what, exactly, does this have to do with the role of prophecy? In fact, literally everything.

When you receive a prophetic promise and when someone shares with you a vision for your own bright future, it can be so very easy to feel as though the future intended will arrive all on its very own. However, you and I have been given a role to play in bringing about the manifestation of our prophetic promises. It is not enough to simply wait, hope, dream, and believe. Faith demands active participation! It demands willingness! Rather than waiting for the manifestation to come, realize that you are always, always contributing to your very own outcomes. Truly, your thoughts are prophesying all throughout any given day.

SECTION THREE

THE DIDACHE

Now concerning spiritual gifts, brethren, I would not have you ignorant.

2 Ye know that ye were Gentiles, carried away unto these dumb idols, even as ye were led.

3 Wherefore I give you to understand, that no man speaking by the Spirit of God calleth Jesus accursed: and that no man can say that Jesus is the Lord, but by the Holy Ghost.

4 Now there are diversities of gifts, but the same Spirit.

5 And there are differences of administrations, but the same Lord.

6 And there are diversities of operations, but it is the same God which worketh all in all.

7 But the manifestation of the Spirit is given to every man to profit withal.

8 For to one is given by the Spirit the word of wisdom; to another the word of knowledge by the same Spirit;

9 To another faith by the same Spirit; to another the gifts of healing by the same Spirit;

10 To another the working of miracles; to another prophecy; to another

discerning of spirits; to another divers kinds of tongues; to another the interpretation of tongues:

11 But all these worketh that one and the selfsame Spirit, dividing to every man severally as he will.

12 For as the body is one, and hath many members, and all the members of that one body, being many, are one body: so also is Christ.

13 For by one Spirit are we all baptized into one body, whether we be Jews or Gentiles, whether we be bond or free; and have been all made to drink into one Spirit.

14 For the body is not one member, but many.

15 If the foot shall say, Because I am not the hand, I am not of the body; is it therefore not of the body?

16 And if the ear shall say, Because I am not the eye, I am not of the body; is it therefore not of the body?

17 If the whole body were an eye, where were the hearing? If the whole were hearing, where were the smelling?

18 But now hath God set the members every one of them in the body, as it hath pleased him.

19 And if they were all one member, where were the body?
20 But now are they many members, yet but one body.

21 And the eye cannot say unto the hand, I have no need of thee: nor again the head to the feet, I have no need of you.

22 Nay, much more those members of the body, which seem to be more feeble, are necessary:

23 And those members of the body, which we think to be less honourable, upon these we bestow more abundant honour; and our uncomely parts have more abundant comeliness.

24 For our comely parts have no need: but God hath tempered the body together, having given more abundant honour to that part which lacked.

25 That there should be no schism in the body; but that the members should have the same care one for another.

26 And whether one member suffer, all the members suffer with it; or one member be honoured, all the members rejoice with it.

27 Now ye are the body of Christ, and members in particular.

28 And God hath set some in the church, first apostles, secondarily prophets, thirdly teachers, after that miracles, then gifts of healings, helps, governments, diversities of tongues.

29 Are all apostles? are all prophets? are all teachers? are all workers of miracles?

30 Have all the gifts of healing? do all speak with tongues? do all interpret?

31 But covet earnestly the best gifts: and yet shew I unto you a more excellent way. (1 Corinthians 12:1-31 KJV)

For centuries, it has been said and taught within Christendom that the role of prophecy was reserved only for the select - only for those who held the office of the prophet. It has been suggested that even in the writings of the Pauline epistles it is said that not all prophesy. This simply is not true, nor has it ever been. The early church did not view prophecy the way in which we, today, view prophecy. Prophecy, to those early believers of the apostolic church, was viewed in a much more universal way, with believers believing wholeheartedly that all who possess the Spirit of Christ can, will, and do possess the power to prophesy. Although there were some who were known to be more vocal or more prominent than others where the gift of prophecy was concerned, the early church did believe that all possessed the power and ability to prophesy - as the Spirit willed it. We find this, also, within the writings of the Didache - a first century writing that details the teachings of the early apostles, outlining customs and traditions.

1. Whosoever then comes and teaches you all these things aforesaid, receive him.

2. But if the teacher himself be perverted and teach another doctrine to destroy these things, do not listen to him, but if his teaching be for the increase of

righteousness and knowledge of the Lord, receive him as the Lord.

3. And concerning the Apostles and Prophets, act thus according to the ordinance of the Gospel.

4. Let every Apostle who comes to you be received as the Lord,

5. But let him not stay more than one day, or if need be a second as well; but if he stay three days, he is a false prophet.

6. And when an Apostle goes forth let him accept nothing but bread till he reach his night's lodging; but if he ask for money, he is a false prophet.

7. Do not test or examine any prophet who is speaking in a spirit, "for every sin shall be forgiven, but this sin shall not be forgiven."

8. But not everyone who speaks in a spirit is a prophet, except he have the behaviour of the Lord. From his

behaviour, then, the false prophet and the true prophet shall be known.

9. And no prophet who orders a meal in a spirit shall eat of it: otherwise he is a false prophet.

10. And every prophet who teaches truth, if he do not what he teaches, is a false prophet.

11. But no prophet who has been tried and is genuine, though he enact a worldly mystery of the Church, if he teach not others to do what he does himself, shall be judged by you: for he has his judgment with God, for so also did the prophets of old.

12. But whosoever shall say in a spirit "Give me money, or something else," you shall not listen to him; but if he tell you to give on behalf of others in want, let none judge him.

XII

1. Let everyone who "comes in the Name of the Lord" be received; but when you have tested him you shall know him, for you shall have understanding of true and false. 2. If he who comes is a traveller, help him as much as you can, but he shall not remain with you more than two days, or, if need be, three. 3. And if he wishes to settle among you and has a craft, let him work for his bread. 4. But if he has no craft provide for him according to your understanding, so that no man shall live among you in idleness because he is a Christian. 5. But if he will not do so, he is making traffic of Christ; beware of such.

XIII

1. But every true prophet who wishes to settle among you is "worthy of his food."
2. Likewise a true teacher is himself worthy, like the workman, of his food.
3. Therefore thou shalt take the firstfruit of the produce of the winepress and of the threshingfloor and of oxen and sheep, and shalt give them as the firstfruits to the prophets, for they are your high priests.
4. But if you have not a prophet, give to the poor.
5. If thou makest bread, take the firstfruits, and give it according to the commandment.
6. Likewise when thou openest a jar of wine or oil, give the firstfruits to the prophets.
7. Of money also and clothes, and of all your possessions, take the firstfruits, as it

seem best to you, and give according to the commandment.

XIV

1. On the Lord's Day of the Lord come together, break bread and hold Eucharist, after confessing your transgressions that your offering may be pure;

2. But let none who has a quarrel with his fellow join in your meeting until they be reconciled, that your sacrifice be not defiled.

3. For this is that which was spoken by the Lord, "In every place and time offer me a pure sacrifice, for I am a great king," saith the Lord, "and my name is wonderful among the heathen."

XV

1. Appoint therefore for yourselves bishops and deacons worthy of the Lord,

meek men, and not lovers of money, and truthful and approved, for they also minister to you the ministry of the prophets and teachers.

2. Therefore do not despise them, for they are your honourable men together with the prophets and teachers.

3. And reprove one another not in wrath but in peace as you find in the Gospel, and let none speak with any who has done wrong to his neighbour, nor let him hear a word from you until he repents.

4. But your prayers and alms and all your acts perform as ye find in the Gospel of our Lord.

XVI

1. "Watch" over your life "let your lamps" be not quenched "and your loins" be not ungirded, but be "ready," for ye

know not "the hour in which our Lord cometh."

2. But be frequently gathered together seeking the things which are profitable for your souls, for the whole time of your faith shall not profit you except ye be found perfect at the last time;

3. For in the last days the false prophets and the corruptors shall be multiplied, and the sheep shall be turned into wolves, and love shall change to hate;

4. For as lawlessness increaseth they shall hate one another and persecute and betray, and then shall appear the deceiver of the world as a Son of God, and shall do signs and wonders and the earth shall be given over into his hands and he shall commit iniquities which have never been since the world began.

5. Then shall the creation of mankind come to the fiery trial and "many shall

be offended" and be lost, but "they who endure" in their faith "shall be saved" by the curse itself.

6. And "then shall appear the signs" of the truth. First the sign spread out in Heaven, then the sign of the sound of the trumpet, and thirdly the resurrection of the dead:

7. But not of all the dead, but as it was said, "The Lord shall come and all his saints with him."

8. Then shall the world "see the Lord coming on the clouds of Heaven."

As is made plain in the text of ancient writings within the first century, the early church regarded prophecy and the role of prophecy in a very natural way - welcoming the function of the prophet into daily life. The role of the prophet was considered so important, in fact, that the early apostles, according to the text of the Didache, had very specific, very detailed protocol concerning prophecy and the role of the prophet. Could it be that the reason the early church walked in such a great measure of the supernatural was because it valued the role of the prophet and also understood the truth concerning the prophetic voice? Might it be that the early church truly did believe that prophecy, like all gifts, exists for all that it is always present, according to the power that worketh in us? It would seem so. All throughout history, we find that where the Spirit is present, so, too, is the gift of prophecy and those who would heed the call of the prophet.

CLOSING THOUGHTS

According to the Encyclopedia Brittanica, concerning prophecy and the role fo the prophet, in its narrower sense, the term prophet (Greek prophētēs, "forthteller") refers to an inspired person who believes that he has been sent by his god with a message to tell. He is, in that sense, the mouthpiece of his god. In a broader sense, the word can refer to anybody who utters the will of a deity, often ascertained through visions, dreams, or the casting of lots; the will of the deity also may be spoken in a liturgical setting. The prophet, thus, is often associated with the priest, the shaman (a religious figure in tribal societies who functions as a healer, diviner, and possessor of psychic powers), the diviner (foreteller), and the mystic.

Nature And Significance

A primary characteristic of prophetic self-consciousness is an awareness of a call, which is regarded as the prophet's legitimization. That call is viewed as coming ultimately from a deity and by means of a dream, a vision, or an audition or through the mediation of another prophet. The Hebrew prophet Jeremiah's call was in the form of a vision, in which he was told by God that he had already been chosen to be a prophet before he was born (Jeremiah 1:5). When the call of the deity is mediated through a prophet who is the master of a prophetic group or an individual follower, such a call can be seen as a mandate. Furthermore, such mediation means that the spirit of the prophet master has been transferred simultaneously to the disciple. In the case of cult prophets, such as the prophets of the gods Baal and Yahweh in ancient Canaan, the call may be regarded as a mandate of the cult.

Prophets were often organized into guilds in which they received their training. The guilds were led by a prophet master, and their members could be distinguished from other members of their society by their garb (such as a special mantle) or by physical marks or grooming (such as baldness, a mark on the forehead, or scars of self-laceration). The nature of prophecy is twofold: either inspired (by visions or revelatory auditions) or acquired (by learning certain techniques). In many cases both aspects are present. The goal of learning certain prophetic techniques is to reach an ecstatic state in which revelations can be received. That state might be reached through the use of music, dancing, drums, violent bodily movement, and self-laceration. The ecstatic prophet is regarded as being filled with the divine spirit, and in that state the deity speaks through him. Ecstatic oracles, therefore, are generally delivered by the prophet in the first-person singular pronoun and are spoken in a short, rhythmic style.

That prophets employing ecstatic techniques have been called madmen is accounted for by descriptions of their loss of control over themselves when they are "possessed" by the deity. Prophets in ecstatic trances often have experienced sensations of corporeal transmigration (as did the 6th-century-BCE Hebrew prophet Ezekiel and the 6th–7th-century-CE founder of Islam, Muhammad). Such prophets are esteemed by coreligionists to have a predisposition for such unusual sensations.

The functions of the prophet and priest occasionally overlap, for priests sometimes fulfill a prophetic function by uttering an oracle of a deity. Such an oracle often serves as part of a liturgy, as when ministers or priests in modern Christian churches read scriptural texts that begin with the proclamation "Thus says the Lord." The priest, in this instance, fulfills the prophetic function of the cult. Not only do the roles of the prophet and priest overlap, but so do the roles of the prophet and shaman. A shaman seldom remembers the message he has delivered when possessed, whereas the prophet always remembers what has happened to him and what he "heard."

As is made obvious, historically, all throughout the ages, mankind has longed to better understand the prophetic realms and to better understand the supernatural dimension. Prophecy, though, has never truly been merely a religious concept - though prophecy is defined in some way, to some degree, by all world religions. Prophecy is much more universal than religion would ever dare to admit. Religion, often, in an attempt to control the masses through the instilling of fear, has often used the prophetic gift with ulterior motive, using prophecy as a means of control and manipulation. When the Body of

Christ, though, begins to become awakened to the reality of the inner realm of the mind, recognizing the power of belief, of thought, and of intention, and when the eyes of understanding become enlightened, as Paul noted, the prophetic gift will become awakened all the more. You see, something truly remarkable begins to happen when a seeker begins to realize that the power to prophesy has always been linked, intrinsically, with the power to create and to form new worlds. According to the text of the sacred scriptures, in the very beginning of ti all, God spoke. However, as I've so often said, long, long before God first spoke, God first thought. God first envisioned. And it was from this thought of God that the creative power of the Godhead first flowed forth.   And, in an instant, a world was formed.

In the beginning God created the heaven and the earth.

2 And the earth was without form, and void; and darkness was upon the face of the deep. And the Spirit of God moved upon the face of the waters.

3 And God said, Let there be light: and there was light.

4 And God saw the light, that it was good: and God divided the light from the darkness.

5 And God called the light Day, and the darkness he called Night. And the

evening and the morning were the first day.

6 And God said, Let there be a firmament in the midst of the waters, and let it divide the waters from the waters. 31 And God saw every thing that he had made, and, behold, it was very good. And the evening and the morning were the sixth day. (Genesis 1:1-6,31 KJV)

In the very beginning of it all, long before the world ever came to be - long before the light first shined through the cosmos, as the Creator uttered those words, there was creative, divine intent. There was vision.   There was a thought that existed in the mind of the Godhead. You were there within that thought. And so was I.   There was no separation. There was no division or sense of dualism or dichotomy. There was no religion, nor was there any need for such child-like, primitive beliefs. There was no consciousness of sin. There was only Union.

In the account of Creation as recorded in the Book of Genesis, we find a great and remarkable correlation between the act of seeing and the act of speaking. When thought is held and when words are spoken, vision is enacted and brought from the realm of the invisible, manifested into the realm of the visible. And the Word becomes flesh - spirit becoming impressed onto the natural world of time and space. Vision, you see, is just as natural a force as it is heavenly. Those visions that you see flooding and racing through the mind's eye all throughout the day and night serve as reminders to you of the power you've always possessed to bring about the life you truly want and desire. The life you desire is the abundant life you've been promised. The time has come to "see" your life in a new and heavenly way. What you call "good" will be exactly that. And what you call "bad" will be as you define it. You and I, though, by divine and intelligent design, having been formed and fashioned in the image and in the likeness of God, have been given the responsibility of defining the world as we choose. We define life as we choose. And all day long, you and I are bringing this definition into reality, according to our thoughts and beliefs.

PROPHETIC
ACTIVATION

To my friends and partners of the ministry, as an added, special bonus for your continued support, I felt inspired by the Holy Spirit to include what I feel to be a needed, useful chapter to share with you the benefits of recognizing your own prophetic power. To date, as of the time of this writing, I have been privileged and honored to have ministered to audiences throughout the world, have written numerous books that have gone on to become bestsellers, and have witnessed, firsthand, the miraculous power of the Holy Spirit at conferences throughout the world.

Through it all, what I have come to witness and become more reminded of each day is that the prophetic gift is a gift of creation. When you activate the prophetic voice, you are, in truth, activating and harnessing the very power that formed the worlds. I wanted to share with you a principle that I shared years ago in my book Creating Your Soul Map. It is the principle of "precision."

You see, it is truly not enough to have vision, alone. It truly is not. We know, according to the text of the Holy Bible, that without vision, we perish. Yet, vision, alone, has never truly been enough to bring about the abundant life you've been promised. You see, my friend and fellow seeker, it isn't enough to have a vision for your own bright future. To bring that future into manifestation in the physical, three-dimensional world of space and time, you must have a clear vision. You must see it more precisely - much more accurately. Precision is required within the Kingdom of Heaven - particularly where the prophetic gift is concerned. Do you want to prophesy, or do you want to prophesy accurately and clearly, with precision? Yes; there is a difference. Anyone can speak words of hope, edification, and faith. However, to bring the future to pass - to actually create the future - you're going to have to, first, begin to become much more precise and much more specific about the future you claim to envision.

And he cometh to Bethsaida; and they bring a blind man unto him, and besought him to touch him.

23 And he took the blind man by the hand, and led him out of the town; and when he had spit on his eyes, and put his hands upon him, he asked him if he saw ought.

24 And he looked up, and said, I see men as trees, walking.

25 After that he put his hands again upon his eyes, and made him look up: and he was restored, and saw every man clearly.

26 And he sent him away to his house, saying, Neither go into the town, nor tell it to any in the town.

27 And Jesus went out, and his disciples, into the towns of Caesarea Philippi: and

by the way he asked his disciples, saying unto them, Whom do men say that I am?

28 And they answered, John the Baptist; but some say, Elias; and others, One of the prophets.

29 And he saith unto them, But whom say ye that I am? And Peter answereth and saith unto him, Thou art the Christ.

30 And he charged them that they should tell no man of him.

31 And he began to teach them, that the Son of man must suffer many things, and be rejected of the elders, and of the chief priests, and scribes, and be killed, and after three days rise again.

32 And he spake that saying openly. And Peter took him, and began to rebuke him.

33 But when he had turned about and looked on his disciples, he rebuked Peter, saying, Get thee behind me, Satan: for thou savourest not the things that be of God, but the things that be of men.

34 And when he had called the people unto him with his disciples also, he said unto them, Whosoever will come after me, let him deny himself, and take up his cross, and follow me. (Mark 8:22-34 KJV)

There truly is much to be said about the importance of vision - the importance of possessing "sight." Vision, though, has always come in many forms. Everyone can see and envision something - even the blind. All possess the power to cast vision, to hope, and to dream. But it's never truly been enough to merely see. One must see clearly. The above passage from the synoptic Gospel of Mark is a reminder that clear vision - clear sight - is essential. But the "sight" goes far, far beyond the mere natural sight of the natural eye. In the Kingdom, the inner sight matters all the more. The realm of the Kingdom of Heaven within is a realm of inner vision - a realm of inner sight. To awaken the power of the prophetic gift residing within you, it is vital that you not only see your own bright future - imagining it - but you must see it clearly. You must see it more accurately and with greater precision.

And so now I would ask, when you envision the future life, what does it look like? Can you see it? More importantly, can you see it clearly? What do the details look like? What do you see when you bring the vision into greater focus? The new home that you dream of, the new career, and the new, more satisfying relationship, what do those things look like? What color are the walls in your dream home, as it flashes onto the screen of your mind's eye? When you envision that first date with your new partner, where will you be going for dinner that evening? And, concerning the new career you imagine and dream of, what will you wear to your first interview?

Details matter. Especially within the Kingdom of Heaven. All of those details - those precise, precise details -

matter more than you may realize. When I felt the inspiration of the Holy host to write what would become the international bestseller The Universe is at Your Command, I felt within my spirit the prophetic voice calling out. The Universe and all of Heaven and Earth are waiting, patiently, for you to use your faith and to make decrees. There's a reason you continue to find yourself daydreaming of the more abundant life - the life you've been promised. The reason, simply, is because long, long before time ever even began and long, long before you ever were formed within the womb of your mother, even then, you were programmed for greatness. Even then, long before the worlds were ever spoken into existence by the voice of God, you were programmed to prosper. The prophetic gift is a universal reminder to all of humanity that we have been infused and instilled with all the power of the Godhead and that what we think, we ultimately are. After all, as the scriptures remind us, as a man thinketh in his heart, so is he.

My friend and fellow seeker, the time has come to begin to become more much more specific where your vision is concerned. The future "You" already exists within the heart and within the mind of God. And that future is good. It is bright. And there are plans to prosper you and not to harm you - to bring you to a place of hope and to an expected end. You have been given a divine and heavenly role to play in all matters of your own life, whether you realize it or not. Nothing has ever been an act of chance or happenstance. It's all - literally everything - been part of a carefully crafted, divinely programmed code. The code is within you even now, and day by day and moment by moment, you are walking out your destiny upon Planet Earth. What you and I have been conditioned to view as merely "everyday life," Heaven views it as "destiny." Understanding this, the prophetic gift becomes awakened all the more and a greater sense of accuracy and precision is ignited within the vision.

ABOUT THE AUTHOR

Dr. Jeremy Lopez is Founder and President of Identity Network and Now Is Your Moment. Identity Network is one of the world's leading prophetic resource sites, offering books, teachings, and courses to a global audience. For more than thirty years, Dr. Lopez has been considered a pioneering voice within the field of the prophetic arts and his proven strategies for success coaching are now being implemented by various training groups and faith groups throughout the world. Dr. Lopez is the author of more than forty books, including his international bestselling books The Universe is at Your Command and Creating with Your Thoughts. Throughout his career, he has spoken prophetically into the lives of heads of business as well as heads of state. He has ministered to Governor Bob Riley of the State of Alabama, Prime Minister Benjamin Netanyahu, and Shimon Peres. Dr. Lopez continues to be a highly sought conference teacher and host, speaking on the topics of human potential and spirituality.

ADDITIONAL WORKS

Prophetic Transformation

The Universe is at Your Command: Vibrating the Creative Side of God

Creating with Your Thoughts

Creating Your Soul Map: Manifesting the Future You with a Vision Board

Creating Your Soul Map: A Visionary Workbook

Abandoned to Divine Destiny

The Law of Attraction: Universal Power of Spirit

Made in the USA
Middletown, DE
20 November 2020

24417440R00050